Can You Hear Me?

A Journey with
the God Who
Speaks

By Craig Farris

ISBN-13: 9798715740915

Cover design by: Art Painter
Library of Congress Control Number: 2018675309
Printed in the United States of America

Introduction

I am an avid reader and get excited every time I get a book. To me, a book is an opportunity to get a glimpse into who the author is. Many times, based on what type of book it is, it can feel like I am sitting at a table having a conversation with the author. I hope this book not only helps you see a piece of who I am, but also provides you with ideas that can lead you into your own encounters with Holy Spirit.

I have made many attempts over the years at writing books, and all of my attempts have ended in frustration. It is actually a bit of a miracle I have finished this one. I tend to write for a while and then make the mistake of going back through and reading it. At which point, I find that I really do not like what I have written and throw it out. Apparently, that is a bad strategy for finishing a book. This book was completed because my wife Shannon knew that if I was going to fulfill the prophetic word that I would write books, then she was going to need to help me.

I had been working two jobs--ninety-plus hours a week. At my day job, I worked at a computer a lot; and since Shannon and I weren't getting much face time, we would send emails. We were also homeschooling so Shannon would regularly send me questions about the Bible or biblical topics. Although Shannon is amazing and creates most of the curriculum our kids use for school, she relies on me to cover Bible topics or exercises outside of devotional times. Sometimes, I also do a little teaching on history because I like history.

One day while I was working, she sent me an email asking questions about the prophetic. I answered her questions not thinking much about them. She then followed my response with another question about some of the activations I have used to practice hearing God. I responded back with several.

Shannon then got my undivided attention when she emailed back with a peculiar question: Do you have thirty activations? Peculiar and odd but not enough to get me to focus long enough to figure out what she was doing.

Later, when I got some downtime, I started writing out the different activations I had used over the years. Surprisingly, there were thirty-plus. Who knew? Once I had sent them to her, I finally figured out what she was doing. After she emailed back and asked if there were scriptures for each activation, I definitely knew. "She has me writing a book!" Shannon knows the word over my life is that I am supposed to write books, manuals, journals, and curriculum and wasn't going to allow something like two jobs and ninety hours a week stop me from pursuing my destiny.

This book is a first step into prophetic fulfillment in an area in which I have only embraced failure. Shannon has fought to help me see the importance of what I teach and the value of cooperation with the prophetic word. We don't get a prophetic word or have a conversation with Holy Spirit to just sit and wait. We must move!

So here we are: me at a moment of fulfilling the prophetic word spoken over me and you, looking to hear God in a new fresh way.

Allow me a moment to express how using these activations have helped me. These can be tools for bettering a gift, but for me I have found that they are keys to exploring and deepening a relationship. Did these help with my gift? Well, in some of the circles I travel, I am known for being highly accurate. However, it is my relationship with Him and the mark of Him on my life that others see that are the fruit of these activations. I love being accurate and what that means for people but it does not compare to being with my Father. He is indescribable, and yet I must speak of Him. I could go on, but, please, discover for yourself how there are no words but you must find some for the, awe, we are invited into.

May the next thirty days or however long you take with this book be some of the most profitable days of your life. May your eyes and ears be opened to see and hear like never before.

Until then, Excelsior -- upward and onward to greater glory!

How to Use This Book

Each day of this book is written so that you read the activation; and with it in mind, you read the following scriptures and corresponding story. Once you have completed the reading, you then do the activation yourself. It is important to journal as you start these exercises.

Many of these exercises became part of my daily life and continue to be. I mention that so you know this book is not just to be rushed through in thirty days but can be an ongoing process. There are also many days that I still do multiple activations as part of my time with Holy Spirit.

Take your time. Journal the ones which are easiest for you and maybe focus only on those for a while. Get used to using that "muscle" regularly and with intentionality and then move on to a new one that might be a little different for you. When I began these activations, I would continue an activation for over a month before trying a new one. Don't be in a rush to move through the activations. These aren't assignments to be completed; they are engagements to create an opportunity for encounter.

To encourage you, all of these felt awkward when I first started, and many times it seemed like I was messing up. Ultimately, as I continued to read scripture and pursue Him in prayer, I found He was in a far greater pursuit of me. I just needed to believe that He was pursuing me, and I was hearing His voice.

Do remember to have fun with this. Don't focus on right or wrong, but focus on the opportunity to build a closer relationship with Him.

Table of Contents

Day 1 - Daily Bread 1

Day 2 - Share the Love 7

Day 3 - Dinner Date 13

Day 4 - Reading with the

                Master Author 19

Day 5 - You've Got Mail 25

Day 6 - Jamming with Jesus 31

Day 7 - First Names First 35

Day 8 - Know the Nameless 41

Day 9 - Say What? 47

Day 10 - What to wear 53

Day 11 - Holy GPS 59

Day 12 - Family Road Trip 65

Day 13 - Heavenly Melody 71

Day 14 - Treasure Hunt 77

Day 15 - Divine Appointments 83

Day 16 - Just Dance 89

Day 17 - Rise and Shine 93

Day 18 - Spot it! 97

Day 19 - Game On 103

Day 20 - The Creator's Thoughts 109

Day 21 - What is on His mind 115

Day 22 - Breaking News! 121

Day 23 - Mountains, Oceans

              and Deserts 127

Day 24 - Just for Fun 133

Day 25 - Holy Spirit art critic 139

Day 26 - A Walk to Remember 143

Day 27 - Movie Night with Dad 147

Day 28 - What's on the Menu 151

Day 29 - World Traveler 157

Day 30 - Getaway 163

Final thoughts

Activations List

About the Author

Stay Connected

Day 1 - Daily Bread

Get your Bible and ask Holy Spirit for a verse for your day.

Hebrews 4:12 (AMPC) "For the Word that God speaks is alive and full of power [making it active, operative, energizing, and effective]; it is sharper than any two-edged sword, penetrating to the dividing line of the breath of life (soul) and [the immortal] spirit, and of joints and marrow [of the deepest parts of our nature], exposing and sifting and analyzing and judging the very thoughts and purposes of the heart."

2 Timothy 3:16-17 (AMPC) "Every Scripture is God-breathed (given by His inspiration) and profitable for instruction, for reproof and conviction of sin, for correction of error and discipline in obedience, [and] for training in righteousness (in holy living, in conformity to God's will in thought, purpose, and action), So that the man of God may be complete and proficient, well fitted and thoroughly equipped for every good work."

As you do this exercise, you'll find you don't always have to be as intentional about asking as you do about paying attention. There are many times I almost miss what He is saying because I gloss over a verse or dismiss a thought. The word is alive and full of power; we have to be more intentional in our lives to recognize and embrace the power of the word. We often read for discipline and not for relationship. Intentional reading and engagement with scripture opens the door to encountering the power of the word and its Author.

Asking for a verse should be an easy thing. I once asked and heard John 11:35—the shortest verse in the Bible-- "Jesus wept."

This is the story of Jesus raising Lazarus from the dead. Prior to raising him, Jesus wept. An amazing story, but I was very confused by why that might be the verse for me that day. I had all kinds of questions. Is someone going to die? Will I raise someone from the dead? Do I need to cry?

Don't worry, I didn't die. What Holy Spirit was doing was giving me an invitation to a conversation. Why did Jesus weep? I began asking questions about other details around that verse? As we talked about it, I felt it was interesting that Jesus probably knew He was going to raise Lazarus from the dead, and yet He wept. I started thinking, what if Jesus began to weep because in the moment of seeing all the mourners, He began to see His own end and knowing what was going to happen to the disciples after He died.

Meditating on those simple two words opened up an incredible opportunity to see something I had never seen before. This verse, combined with the conversation set the tone for my day. I engaged my day looking for what was in front of me while being aware of what was to come. The power of scripture changes everything internally and externally.

Day 1 Journaling

Get your Bible and ask for a verse for your day. (Meditate on it)

Write about your encounter below.

_____

_____

_____

_____

_____

_____

_____

_____

_____

_____

Day 2 - Share the Love

Get your Bible and ask Holy Spirit for a verse for a friend or family member.

Isaiah 40:8 (ESV) "The grass withers, the flower fades, but the word of our God will stand forever."

Matthew 24:35 (AMPC) "Sky and earth will pass away, but My words will not pass away."

I once needed a financial miracle--the kind of miracle that feeds and houses my family. As I began to pray in my bed at the break of a new day, a name popped into my head. The name was of someone I hadn't talked with in months. As I shifted from praying for my finances to praying for the individual, I heard; Isaiah 43:19 - "...I am doing a new thing..."

I wasn't sure what that meant or if I should contact them to share the verse. So, I continued to pray and looked up the verse to make sure I had the right "address" connected to the verse I was hearing. Sure enough it was correct.

Now I had to make the shift from praying and hearing to giving. I sent a message to the person with the verse but received no answer. I figured it didn't mean anything to this person since there wasn't an answer, and I went on about my day. A few days later, I got a reply that they had just seen the message, and it was confirmation to another word they had just received.

Then within days, miracles, food and home were taken care of. For many people it would seem that releasing a word to a friend had nothing to do with the miracles of my rent being paid and food being brought to my door, but we serve an incredible God who likes to do things that appear to be out of order or disjointed. I didn't know when I had sent the word to my friend that it was the key to unlocking our families' needed miracles. I just was trying to be a blessing to my friend and obedient to my King. However, being obedient has a way of breaking open windows of miracles and favor.

A verse can change everything; a person, a business, or a family. Take a chance.

Day 2 Journaling

Get your Bible and ask Holy Spirit for a verse for a friend or family member.

Write about your encounter below.

_____

_____

_____

_____

_____

_____

_____

_____

_____

_____

Day 3 - Dinner Date

Have a meal with Holy Spirit. Set a place and expect to have a conversation like you would if your friend was sitting at the table with you.

Psalms 23:5 (NKJV) "You prepare a table before me in the presence of my enemies, you anoint my head with oil, my cup runs over."

David understood that in His presence, nothing could touch him; and that from the place of friendship, he would walk away from that encounter completely different. Therefore, as you invite the Holy Spirit to join you in a meal, you are asking for a relational upgrade.

Luke 24:30 (NKJV) "Now it came to pass, as He sat at the table with them, that He took bread, blessed and broke it, and gave it to them. Then their eyes were opened and they knew Him."

In this verse you see that those that were at the table with Him received the revelation of who they were with. Sitting at the table opens a door to see aspects of GOD you wouldn't see any other way.

I have practiced this ever since I heard Graham Cooke's message on Psalm 23 and how there is nothing like eating watermelon in the midst of a battle. (I actually say watermelon. Graham said melon.) From Psalms 23 passage, I develop my picture, where I envision eating watermelon. Now, come on, who wouldn't want to be eating watermelon in the middle of a battle? The idea of being in the middle of a battle and being untouchable while in such a state of peace is powerful; you can eat watermelon, be at peace, and still hold a conversation with GOD.

On many occasions I have been intentional about preparing a place for Holy Spirit to join me for a meal. I have found that in these times I am acutely aware of His presence and find myself wanting to know Him more than when I started to prepare. An incredible byproduct of time with Him is a desire for more time with Him.

One of the ways I have been intentional is actually pulling out a chair for Him to sit in and even setting a cup at that spot. This is not necessary but I have found that sometimes creating a natural atmosphere of invitation helps me engage with the supernatural.

Day 3 Journaling

Have a meal with Holy Spirit. Set a place and expect to have a conversation like you would if your friend was sitting at the table with you.

Write about your encounter below.

_____

_____

_____

_____

_____

_____

_____

_____

_____

_____

_____

Day 4 - Reading with the Master Author

Ask Holy Spirit what to read and read it together.

Jeremiah 36:14-15 (NKJV) "Therefore all the princes sent Jehudi the son of Nethaniah, the son of Shelemiah, the son of Cushi, to Baruch, saying, "Take in your hand the scroll from which you have read in the hearing of the people, and come." So Baruch the son of Neriah took the scroll in his hand and came to them. 15 And they said to him, "Sit down now, and read it in our hearing." So Baruch read it in their hearing."

2 Timothy 4:13 (NKJV) "Bring the cloak that I left with Carpus at Troas when you come—and the books, especially the parchments."

Reading is very enjoyable for me. I grew up reading comic books and then transitioned to books. I remember being about seven when I read my first autobiography. It was about a man named George Mueller. Reading that book was the first time I had felt as though I was not reading alone. Somehow, heaven was in the room with me. As I read about George Mueller, I had a strong sense that not only was I not alone but that parts of what I was reading were to become part of who I would be someday.

Before I reached the age of twelve, I had read this book more than a dozen times. Each time, the same thing happened. The weird thing was that after reading it, I would feel as though I needed to read it again. When I did, different parts of the book or George Mueller's life would be highlighted to me. That time in my life had left a mark on me and has been a guide for the rest of my life.

There have been many books I have been led to read throughout my life, and my time reading has always had unique significance. I have enjoyed each time because I was never reading alone.

Day 4 Journaling

Ask Holy Spirit what to read and read it together.

Write about your encounter below.

_____

_____

_____

_____

_____

_____

_____

_____

_____

_____

_____

Day 5 - You've Got Mail

Ask Holy Spirit what will be the next type of communication you will receive: a phone call, text message, email, Facebook message, etc.?

Samuel 9:15-17 (AMPC) "Now a day before Saul came, the Lord had revealed to Samuel in his ear, Tomorrow about this time I will send you a man from the land of Benjamin, and you shall anoint him to be leader over My people Israel; and he shall save them out of the hand of the Philistines. For I have looked upon the distress of My people, because their cry has come to Me. When Samuel saw Saul, the Lord told him, There is the man of whom I told you. He shall have authority over My people."

Luke 2:10-12 (AMPC) "But the angel said to them, Do not be afraid; for behold, I bring you good news of a great joy which will come to all the people. For to you is born this day in the town of David a Savior, Who is Christ (the Messiah) the Lord! And this will be a sign for you [by which you will recognize Him]: you will find after searching] a Baby wrapped in swaddling clothes and lying in a manger."

Nowadays, since every type of communication is on my phone, I find myself not being as disciplined with what type of communication I am going to receive, (Messenger, text, Marco Polo, etc.) but I know when to look at my phone. I can't tell you the number of times I say to Shannon, "I have to answer this," and she responds, "Answer what?" Then my phone rings. I'm still practicing knowing who is sending the message or calling, and I don't get it right every time. I am learning the difference between a feeling or a guess and when Holy Spirit is giving me a name.

This is an easy low risk exercise that you can do all day, every day. To help you with keeping track, put the information you get in the notes on your phone. Start watching how well you are doing and look for any differences between right and wrong outcomes. Notice what you felt or thought when you got it right versus when you got it wrong.

Day 5 Journaling

Ask Holy Spirit what will be the next type of communication you will receive: a phone call, text message, email, Facebook message, etc.?

Write about your encounter below.

_____

_____

_____

_____

_____

_____

_____

_____

_____

_____

Day 6 - Jamming with Jesus

Ask Holy Spirit what song will be on the radio when you get in the car.

Ephesians 5:19 (AMPC) "Speak out to one another in psalms and hymns and spiritual songs, offering praise with voices and instruments] and making melody with all your heart to the Lord,"

Psalm 32:7 (NLT) "For you are my hiding place; you protect me from trouble. You surround me with songs of victory."

I'm sure by now you realize that we not only serve God, but we also need to have a relationship with our Friend, with Truth; and what relationship do you have that doesn't involve fun? If you're in one, get out of it. Our Creator is not boring or above real interactions. He desires us to want, need, and fight for interactions with Him.

It is an incredible experience to get into your car and hear a song that the lyrics seem to be sent directly from heaven to you. As if, you are being serenaded by your Love. A message from His lips to your heart. This experience can change your life.

This activation is about expanding our perception of how He can speak to us. That we can hear what will be playing and also the message in it. I have even asked Him if we could listen to a specific song together and then what channel to find it on. Just like I would ask my friend if he wanted to watch the baseball game and if he knew what channel it was on. Our Father is looking to spend time having fun with His children.

Day 6 Journaling

Ask Holy Spirit what song will be on the radio when you get in the car.

Write about your encounter below.

_____

_____

_____

_____

_____

_____

_____

_____

_____

_____

_____

_____

Day 7 - First Names First

Ask Holy Spirit who will be the first person you see today?

Jeremiah 33:3 (NKJV) "Call to Me, and I will answer you, and show you great and mighty things, which you do not know."

John 10:27 (NKJV) "My sheep hear My voice, and I know them, and they follow Me."

Everyday should begin with a conversation with Holy Spirit. As you get into the habit of talking to Him first, you can then move into asking about details of the day ahead. I used to ask all the time about who would be the first person I would run into at work. As I got better at hearing, then I would begin to ask more specific questions. What would they be wearing? Would something be different about them? Or, I would ask God to highlight anything about them that I wouldn't be able to guess without "insider" information.

There have been occasions when I have actually texted the person I believed I would see first thing that day and asked what they were wearing. This was so I wouldn't live in any kind of doubt that I had just guessed it when I saw them. It can be life changing for those who don't know Jesus to get a random text asking if they are wearing their Scooby shirt today.

When I began this activation I was more worried about right and wrong than the relational aspect of this conversation. When I realized how important it can be for a person to know that God was talking about them to someone else, this became a different activation. It was no longer about me being right but someone else being known. As I began to understand the importance of this activation it was then that I discovered it could be fun. That it wasn't about being right or creating a life changing moment but that it was about my relationship with Him being demonstrated by sharing our conversation with someone else. Just like hanging out with my best friend and sharing stories Holy Spirit likes to share too. It's just that when He shares it's an opportunity to grow in relationship with Him and to help create an encounter for someone else.

You see, He wants to talk to us as much as we want to hear Him. When we begin to be intentional about listening to Him as much as we talk to, or at Him, our world will begin to change.

Day 7 Journaling

Ask Holy Spirit who will be the first person you see today?

Write about your encounter below.

_____

_____

_____

_____

_____

_____

_____

_____

_____

_____

_____

Day 8 - Know the Nameless

Before you go out for coffee, a snack, lunch or dinner, ask Holy Spirit for the server's gender, age or name.

Mark 14:13-16 (NKJV) "And He sent out two of His disciples and said to them, "Go into the city, and a man will meet you carrying a pitcher of water; follow him. Wherever he goes in, say to the master of the house, 'The Teacher says, "Where is the guest room in which I may eat the Passover with My disciples?"'" Then he will show you a large upper room, furnished and prepared; they make ready for us." So His disciples went out, and came into the city, and found it just as He had said to them; and they prepared the Passover."

Acts 9:11-12 "So the Lord said to him, "Arise and go to the street called Straight, and inquire at the house of Judas for one called Saul of Taurus, for behold, he is praying. And in a vision he has seen a man named Ananias coming in and putting his hand on him, so that he might receive his sight."

I do this activation with my kids when we use a drive thru. As we pull into a place and order, I will ask the kids if they have any information about the individual that will be taking our order. Then we do the same for the individual taking our cash and the one who will hand us our order.

If you have ever gone through a drive through, you know it may be the same person serving you all the way through, but sometimes, you can have up to six different people. In a restaurant setting, it is the same. Before we enter, I will ask if a guy or girl will seat us. And go through the whole thing. Will there only be one server? What are the names of anyone we will come in contact with.

I remember one time I asked that question, and we got all the way to the end of our meal, and we hadn't seen the name one of our kids had chosen. Then on our way to the car, there was a friend of ours walking in who had the same name our kid had received.

This activation is the training ground for encounters like Ananias and Saul. (Acts 9:10-19) We want to build the confidence in hearing His voice so that when the opportunity arises we are prepared to see our Saul's become Paul's.

Giving a word to someone who is waiting on you to change their life can have the same life changing impact on you by giving it. We are practicing for the benefit of others as much as for our own benefit.

Always enjoy the adventure, and remember, it's never over until it's over.

Day 8 Journaling

Before you go out for coffee, a snack, lunch or dinner, ask Holy Spirit for the server's gender, age or name.

Write about your encounter below.

_____

_____

_____

_____

_____

_____

_____

_____

_____

_____

_____

Day 9 - Say What?

If you have a meeting or are going out with a friend, ask
Holy Spirit the first thing they will say?

John 1:47-51 (NKJV) "Jesus saw Nathanael coming toward Him, and said of him, "Behold, an Israelite indeed, in whom there is no deceit!" Nathanael said to Him, "How do You know me?" Jesus answered and said to him, "Before Philip called you, when you were under the fig tree, I saw you." Nathanael answered and said to Him, "Rabbi, You are the Son of God! You are the King of Israel!" Jesus answered and said to him, "Because I said to you, 'I saw you under the fig tree,' do you believe? You will see greater things than these." And He said to him, "Most assuredly, I say to you, hereafter you shall see heaven open, and the angels of God ascending and descending upon the Son of Man."

John 4:15-19 (NKJV)"The woman said to Him, "Sir, give me this water, that I may not thirst, nor come here to draw." Jesus said to her, "Go, call your husband, and come here."The woman answered and said, "I have no husband." Jesus said to her, "You have well said, 'I have no husband,' for you have had five husbands, and the one whom you now have is not your husband; in that you spoke truly." The woman said to Him, "Sir, I perceive that You are a prophet."

This exercise is like having an inside secret. This is one exercise that reminds me that He is always with me and that everything I do is important to Him

For a time I had a job that provided me the chance to work with different people on a daily basis without me knowing who it would be. This was a perfect opportunity to be able to ask who I would be with that day and what they would say first. Most times, I would get what they were going to say and the topic of an area in their life that needed a breakthrough. Each time this happened, I found myself in a place knowing how much the individual meant to Him and also that I had a Friend who cares about everything I do.

Day 9 Journaling

If you have a meeting or are going out with a friend, ask Holy Spirit the first thing they will say?

Write about your encounter below.

_____

_____

_____

_____

_____

_____

_____

_____

_____

_____

_____

Day 10 - What to Wear?

Before you get dressed each day, ask Holy Spirit what clothes you should wear then watch for something about your outfit to be mentioned during the day.

Genesis 3:21 (NKJV) "For Adam and his wife the Lord God made tunics of skin and clothed them."

God has had purpose for clothing since the day He clothed Adam and Eve. Think about the specifics of how the priests were dressed or Joseph's coat. There are many examples in scripture as well as in history of how God has used clothing to invite people into their destiny or to introduce Himself to others. This exercise is an easy way to invite Holy Spirit into your everyday life and work in cooperation with Him to see things happen on earth as it is in heaven.

This is an exercise that I don't practice every day anymore. Although recently as I have been more intentional about what I wear out, I have found Holy Spirit wanting to be involved in that decision again.

Recently, I was going out to meet a friend, and when I went to get dressed, I felt like I was to wear a specific superhero t-shirt and tennis shoes During this time, I had been focused on trying to dress more professionally and hadn't worn a t-shirt out of the house in over eight months, so this was quite weird to have this impression. Since this wasn't part of my routine anymore, I was worried I might just be making it up. I argued with myself for a bit about it and then went ahead with the impression I had had.

When I got to where I was meeting my friend, he was still meeting with someone, but they invited me into their conversation. Almost immediately, they began to prophesy over me, starting with what I was wearing! Who knew that a superhero t-shirt and tennis shoes could open a door for a prophetic word? Wild. I wore something that to me made no sense but that ultimately released a word that directly spoke to my identity and a coming breakthrough in my life.

It isn't always a life changing event when I follow what I believe I'm supposed to wear. Sometimes it is as simple as a compliment on the clothing from someone unknown to me or someone that wouldn't typically give a compliment. I just try to practice hearing. I encourage you to journal and track encounters that take place as you start this process.

Day 10 Journaling

Before you get dressed each day, ask Holy Spirit what clothes you should wear then watch for something about your outfit to be mentioned during the day.

Write about your encounter below.

_____

_____

_____

_____

_____

_____

_____

_____

_____

_____

Day 11 - Holy GPS

Go for a drive and ask God where to go.

Psalm 32:8 (NKJV) "I will instruct you and teach you in the way you should go; I will guide you with My eye."

Proverbs 20:24 (AMPC) "Man's steps are ordered by the Lord…"

1 Samuel 16:4 (NASB) "And Samuel did what the Lord said, and came to Bethlehem…"

Many years ago, as I was coming down the stairs in our house, I heard a knock at the door. Our front door had a large piece of glass, and I could see an older gentleman on the other side. I didn't recognize the man until I opened the door; it was not who I expected. Bill Holland was at my door. Bill was an acquaintance of my mother's, who I avoided at all costs. Although Bill has since become a spiritual father to me, at that time around 1994, he scared the crap out of me! He knew things, said things that made me very nervous, and brought conviction just by the atmosphere that came with him. To this day, I have met or seen few people who walk in a relationship with God like Bill. Nor have I found those with such accuracy in discernment and the prophetic like Bill.

When I opened the door, Bill didn't know or recognize me. I asked if I could help him, and he said: "I'm not sure, Son. The Lord told me to come here and knock on this door, but he didn't say why. I'm just going to ask Him again and see what we need to do." PANIC!

What would you do? I had no idea what was happening, and now Bill was telling me God gave him my address. What the heck?

As I was about to slam the door and run for my bat, my mom walked into view. Bill saw her and said, "Sister Teresa, I am here to help get rid of the depression you are battling."

WHAT!? My mom invited Bill in, and he said all kinds of things he shouldn't have known and walked my mom through several things during his time there. When he left, my mother was completely full of joy and happiness.

Sometimes obedience, even what may seem crazy, can save a life. Will you go where He says? Will you trust that He is leading you? Have fun, and who knows, maybe we will end up in the same place.

Day 11 Journaling

Go for a drive and ask God where to go.

Write about your encounter below.

_____

_____

_____

_____

_____

_____

_____

_____

_____

_____

Day 12 - Family Road Trip

Ask Holy Spirit to go on a ride with you and just drive and talk.

John 14:16 (AMPC) "And I will ask the Father, and He will give you another Comforter (Counselor, Helper, Intercessor, Advocate, Strengthener, and Standby), that He may remain with you forever"

John 14:26 (ESV) "But the Helper, the Holy Spirit, whom the Father will send in My name, He will teach you all things, and bring to your remembrance all things that I said to you."

2 Corinthians 13:14 (AMPC) "The grace (favor and spiritual blessing) of the Lord Jesus Christ and the love of God and the presence and fellowship (the communion and sharing together, and participation) in the Holy Spirit be with you all."

Holy Spirit will teach me and bring to remembrance things He has said? Who doesn't want to be taught by Holy Spirit, He who knows the mind of God? What have I forgotten that Jesus once said that I needed to remember? Being taught and remembering, are two incredible opportunities to interact with Holy Spirit.

I have found myself many times needing to find something to hold on to. Something that would provide any hope in the situation I was going through. As I have engaged in conversation with Holy Spirit, I have been reminded of prophetic words spoken over me, scriptures that in their very essence breathed hope into my being. Understanding who I am and the purpose I was created for comes from those very chats I'm suggesting you take.

If I go for a trip with my best friend, part of what is amazing about the trip is being together. Words are optional. As we develop a closer relationship with the ONE who resides within us, we find words become optional and being together is the best part. You can only arrive at words that are optional by having used your words to build that experience and relationship.

Day 12 Journaling

Ask Holy Spirit to go on a ride with you and just drive and talk.

Write about your encounter below.

_____

_____

_____

_____

_____

_____

_____

_____

_____

_____

Day 13 - Heavenly Melody

Put on some worship music and ask God let you hear the worship of heaven.

J ohn 4:24 (NKJV) "God is Spirit, and those who worship Him must worship in spirit and truth."

Revelation 5:11-12 (NKJV) "Then I looked, and I heard the voice of many angels around the throne, the living creatures, and the elders; and the number of them was ten thousand times ten thousand, and thousands of thousands, 12 saying with a loud voice: "Worthy is the Lamb who was slain To receive power and riches and wisdom, And strength and honor and glory and blessing!""

Revelation 7:11 (NKJV) "All the angels stood around the throne and the elders and the four living creatures, and fell on their faces before the throne and worshiped God,"

There are many times as I worship, I begin to tune my ear to the song or sound of heaven. The majority of the time, I hear my Father or Jesus singing over me words of encouragement, pleasure, pride and love--words I thought were about Him.

WayMaker, an incredible song written by Michael W. Smith seems to be everywhere and becoming many individuals' and churches' theme song. One Sunday morning service as we were singing

WayMaker, something began to happen. We got to the part of the song when we sing

WayMaker,

Miracle Worker,

Promise Keeper,

Light in the darkness,

My God

That is who You are.

The interesting thing is I heard someone singing the lyrics really close to me. Now, I was on the front row, and people usually are not that close without me knowing it. As I looked around, there was not anyone close enough for me to be able to hear them that clearly. I continued to sing and then I heard the voice again. This time I got quiet and just listened.

The voice was beautifully unique. As I intently listened, Holy Spirit said, "This is what the Father has heaven singing over you." I started to question that statement, and the voice started to fade. I immediately stopped thinking about the question and said, "Thank you. As I continued listening, it got to the part of My God, that is who You are. I heard Father say, "My son, that is who you are."

Now when I hear that song, I just hear Him singing those words over me. This is easy to practice: as we listen to the worship songs, change the words that are directed to God and hear them sung by God and directed to us. We know His voice. We just need to be intentional about listening.

Day 13 Journaling

Put on some worship music and ask God let you hear the worship of heaven.

Write about your encounter below.

_____

_____

_____

_____

_____

_____

_____

_____

_____

_____

_____

Day 14 - Treasure Hunt

Go to a store with numbered aisles and ask God what aisle to go to and who will be there. Ask for details about the person: man, woman, old, young. This exercise has many options for you to experiment with.

Jeremiah 1:7 (NKJV) "But the Lord said to me: "Do not say, 'I am a youth,' For you shall go to all to whom I send you, And whatever I command you, you shall speak."

Acts 10:4-6 (PHILLIPS) "He stared at the angel in terror, and said, "What is it, Lord?" The angel replied, "Your prayers and your deeds of charity have gone up to Heaven and are remembered before God. Now send men to Joppa for a man called Simon, who is also known as Peter. He is staying as a guest with another Simon, a tanner, whose house is down by the sea."

As I write this, I am at my kitchen table, sitting next to my wife of twenty-five years. When we first met, we would spend hours talking on the phone, writing notes, and just walking and talking. During this time, we learned all kinds of things about each other: where we were born. what each other's hobbies were, favorite foods and movies. However, the most important thing we learned was the sound of each other's voice.

That is the point of this exercise: to learn the sound of His voice. As you practice this, understand that if you get it wrong it is the same as if you misunderstand a person you just met. You just have to ask a person to repeat what they said or for clarification. You would do the same with Holy Spirit. If you ask for who you will see next and you get a man but the next aisle there is a woman, don't be discouraged, think about how you got your answer and try again. If you get it right the next time, what was different? This is about learning the sound of His voice, not about right and wrong. Get excited not just about getting it right but about hearing Him. So go with boldness and know that you are not alone. Relationship with God and the sound of His voice can only be built by making time to listen.

Day 14 Journaling

Go to a store with numbered aisles and ask God what aisle to go to and who will be there. Ask for details about the person: man, woman, old, young. This exercise has many options for you to experiment with.

Write about your encounter below.

_____

_____

_____

_____

_____

_____

_____

_____

_____

Day 15 - Divine Appointments

Ask Holy Spirit for a message for a specific person you will come in contact with today.

Acts 9:10-11 (NKJV) "Now there was a certain disciple at Damascus named Ananias; and to him the Lord said in a vision, "Ananias."And he said, "Here I am, Lord."11 So the Lord said to him, "Arise and go to the street called Straight, and inquire at the house of Judas for one called Saul of Tarsus, for behold, he is praying."

Acts 8:26-29 (NKJV) "26 Now an angel of the Lord spoke to Philip, saying, "Arise and go toward the south along the road which goes down from Jerusalem to Gaza." This is desert. 27 So he arose and went...... 29 Then the Spirit said to Philip, "Go near and overtake this chariot."

For many years, my morning prayer started and ended with, "Where do You want to go and who are we going to talk to?" I have had numerous experiences with being led to specific places and people with a message for them. Part of asking the above question is the commitment to change plans or direction when necessary.

Many years ago, I was working as a janitor at my church. I was running late one day, (In my younger days I really was not good at understanding priorities and commitments.) so I ran out of the house carrying my socks and shoes to the car. As I started to leave the court where I lived, there was a young man walking through the court headed in the direction of the park. God said to stop and tell him that where he was going was going to get him imprisoned.

After speaking with this young man for several minutes, I was able to convince him that not only had I never met him or anyone else in his family, but the information I had for him was from God.

Asking where to go and who to talk to can lead to life changing adventures. That young man did turn around and go the other way.

Enjoy the adventure.

Day 15 Journaling

Ask Holy Spirit for a message for a specific person you will come in contact with today.

Write about your encounter below.

_____

_____

_____

_____

_____

_____

_____

_____

_____

_____

_____

Day 16 - Just Dance

Put on some music and ask God for a dance.

Samuel 6:14-16 (NKJV) "Then David danced before the Lord with all his might; and David was wearing a linen ephod. So David and all the house of Israel brought up the ark of the Lord with shouting and with the sound of the trumpet. Now as the ark of the Lord came into the City of David, Michal, Saul's daughter, looked through a window and saw King David leaping and whirling before the Lord; and she despised him in her heart."

Exodus 15:20-21 (NASB) "Miriam the prophetess, Aaron's sister, took the timbrel in her hand, and all the women went out after her with timbrels and with dancing. Miriam answered them,"Sing to the Lord, for He is highly exalted; The horse and his rider He has hurled into the sea."

When was the last time you danced?

There is a breakthrough that takes place as we begin to dance before the Lord. Deep within our soul, hidden pieces begin to wake up, and we begin to move into a fresh state of joy and victory.

The interesting thing about asking for a dance is stepping into an encounter with Him. We create an opportunity to engage with Holy Spirit in a new way. Many times when I do this, it's not so much that He is dancing with me but being present with me as I dance. Both types of encounters create a place of hope and life.

If you are in a place that you need breakthrough or just need to step into a fun, joyful place, dance with Him.

Day 16 Journaling

Put on some music and ask God for a dance.

Write about your encounter below.

_____

_____

_____

_____

_____

_____

_____

_____

_____

_____

Day 17 - Rise and Shine

Start your morning by saying out loud "Good Morning" and wait for His response.

Numbers 6:24-26 (AMPC) "The Lord bless you and watch, guard, and keep you; The Lord make His face to shine upon and enlighten you and be gracious (kind, merciful, and giving favor) to you; The Lord lift up His [approving] countenance upon you and give you peace (tranquility of heart and life continually)."

Psalm 145:18-19 (NKJV) "The Lord is near to all who call upon Him, To all who call upon Him in truth. He will fulfill the desire of those who fear Him; He also will hear their cry and save them."

Matthew 7:7 (NKJV) "Ask, and it will be given to you; seek, and you will find; knock, and it will be opened to you."

Is there a better way to start the day? I have found myself lost in conversation with God just from waking up and saying "Good Morning." It was as if He had sat on the edge of my bed, waiting for me to wake up so we could talk. Other times, it is just the stillness of His presence that brings me into the depths of who He is.

You see, Holy Spirit's response sets the tone for what comes next. What comes next can be prayer, study time, plans for the day or next month, or even something significant for the rest of your life— all from a "Good Morning."

Day 17 Journaling

Start your morning by saying out loud "Good Morning" and wait for His response.

Write about your encounter below.

_____

_____

_____

_____

_____

_____

_____

_____

_____

_____

Day 18 - Spot It!

Go to a public place and ask God what His favorite thing is about this place.

Psalm 37:28 (NKJV) "For the Lord loves justice, And does not forsake His saints; They are preserved forever,..."

John 3:16 (NASB) "For God so loved the world, that He gave His only begotten Son, that whoever believes in Him shall not perish, but have eternal life."

Romans 5:8 (NKJV) "But God demonstrates His own love toward us, in that while we were still sinners, Christ died for us."

So, with some of these, it's hard to tell a story or give examples without ruining it for you. Let me just say that this one is full of surprises and smiles. When you engage with the One who created everything, it becomes fascinating what gets His attention.

Think about it like this: when Jesus walked the earth, did He stop and interact with everyone? He did not. The choices He made for His inner circle of twelve disciples created an interesting and eclectic group of men. Then there was Nicodemus who met with Jesus in secret. Why was Nicodemus special? Zacchaeus was also a ridiculous choice for a lunch date in that time period or even today.

Have you ever considered the Garden of Gethsemane? What grabbed Jesus attention in that garden? Was there anything special about it? A tree, a row of flowers, or possibly the way the sun came up over the garden?

In 2 Kings 2, when Elijah was taken to heaven, why that particular spot? Was it beautiful because of the water nearby? Did He have a favorite rock there? Anything is possible.

To get a glimpse of what catches His attention is always informative; but more than anything, it is a fascinating fun adventure.

Day 18 Journaling

Go to a public place and ask God what His favorite thing is about this place.

Write about your encounter below.

_____

_____

_____

_____

_____

_____

_____

_____

_____

_____

_____

Day 19 - Game on!

Play a game together: video game, phone game, or board game.

Ecclesiastes 3:4 (ESV) "A time to weep, and a time to laugh; a time to mourn, and a time to dance;"

Psalm 150:4 (NKJV) "Praise Him with the timbrel and dance; Praise Him with stringed instruments and flutes!"

Matthew 28:20 (NKJV) "teaching them to observe all things that I have commanded you; and lo, I am with you always, even to the end of the age." Amen."

First, allow me to clarify: video, phone, or board games are not in scripture. The verses I chose above speak to understanding there is a time for laughter and dancing. If that is so, then what makes us laugh and dance? Praise in its purest form requires an abandon of personal decorum, and He has promised to be with us always. Video games will not chase Him away. So, although games are not in scripture, the One who wrote the scriptures, designed me, and wants to be with me is also the One who placed the creativity within those who created the games I play. That means, video games are a possibility of being together.

One of my most amazing encounters with God was also during the most grueling time in my life. We were living in Arizona, and I was working three jobs which was pushing my working time to a hundred hours a week. It was a crazy time. As you can imagine my prayer life was non-existent. It was all I could do to stay semi-functional. I'm so thankful for the people that helped me through that time.

So, at night, in between jobs, instead of sleeping, I decided to play video games for thirty minutes and then go to work. As I started the game, the air in the room changed, and I felt a familiar presence. I looked to my right, and it was as if I could see Jesus. He was looking at me and said, "I love you." My response did not rise to the occasion as I replied, "Where is my money?"

His arrival to say He loved me was nice, but I had real issues to deal with. We had this short exchange, and He sat with me as I played my game and I wept. He just waited with me, and then I said, "I love you, too." At that moment, He left. I had not understood the depth of His love for me until this encounter.

So many times since then, I have sat down to play video games and have asked Him to sit and play with me. I have never had a time where a second player came into the game, but I have never been alone when I have asked Him to join me. I can always feel His presence with me as I play.

Day 19 Journaling

Play a game together: video game, phone game, or board game.

Write about your encounter below.

_____

_____

_____

_____

_____

_____

_____

_____

_____

_____

Day 20 - The Creator's Thoughts

Ask God, "What do you think about me?"

Jeremiah 29:11 "For I know the thoughts I think toward you, says the Lord, thoughts of peace and not of evil, to give you a future and a hope."

Psalm 139:16-17 "Your eyes saw my substance, being yet unformed. And in Your book they all were written, the days fashioned for me, when as yet there were none of them. How precious also are Your thoughts to me, O God! How great is the sum of them!"

Matthew 10:29-31 "Are not two sparrows sold for a copper coin? And not one of them falls to the ground apart from your Father's will. But the very hairs of your head are all numbered. Do not fear therefore; you are of more value than many sparrows."

Romans 8:28-29. "And we know that all things work together for good to those who love God, to those who are the called, according to His purpose. For whom He foreknew, He also predestined to be conformed to the image of His Son, that He might be the firstborn among many brethren"

We tend to forget how often His thoughts are truly towards us and about us. As we embrace our position in Him, it allows us to expand our capability to understand His thoughts towards others. Many times, when I have done this exercise, I have found myself with scriptures popping into my head.

In 1999, seven years after my dad had died, I found myself asking God about how He was my Father since my dad was now gone. I was curious about what my dad would have said about my life; and if God was my Father now, what did He think? During that dialogue, He said some very specific things about me, one of which was how much He enjoyed being my Father.

Within weeks of Him saying that to me, I was in a Sunday morning service, and a guest speaker began to prophesy over me. One thing he said to me was how much God enjoyed being my Father. Since that word in 1999, I rarely go a day without having a conversation with my Father. My heart changed in a moment of encounter with Him from broken pieces to a whole heart totally committed to Him.

Day 20 Journaling

Ask God, "What do you think about me?"

Write about your encounter below.

_____

_____

_____

_____

_____

_____

_____

_____

_____

_____

Day 21 - What is on His Mind?

Sit in a comfortable spot and ask God what He is thinking about right now.

Amos 4:13 (NASB) "For behold, He who forms mountains and creates the wind And declares to man what are His thoughts, He who makes dawn into darkness And treads on the high places of the earth, The LORD God of hosts is His name."

1 Corinthians 2:16 (KJV) "For who has known the mind of the Lord that he may instruct Him?" But we have the mind of Christ."

It can be challenging for the most imaginative person to come up with what God might be thinking; however, according to I Cor. 2:16, we are given access to the mind of Christ. We are invited to put it on and explore. Allow yourself to go beyond your preconceived idea of what He should be thinking about you, and shift to what He wants to share with you.

Many years ago when I first started this exercise, I would get frustrated because I wasn't getting anything. I finally realized that the problem was that I was asking but not really making room for Him to talk about whatever He wanted to say. Once I came to understand I was asking a question that I didn't want a real answer to, it prepared me to hear whatever He wanted to say.

Psalms 139: 17-18 are a couple verses that speak to what might be on His mind: "How precious and weighty also are Your thoughts to me, O God! How vast is the sum of them! If I could count them, they would be more in number than the sand. When I awoke, I would still be with You."

His thoughts towards me outnumber the sands!

However, this was not the verse I was thinking of many years ago when I sat down in our family room to ask Holy Spirit what He was thinking about. I heard (internal voice) Him say, "I love you." I wasn't sure what to think about what I was hearing. Was I imagining it? Was it just me? I was not sure how "I love you" fit with "What are You thinking?" I was absolutely confused. All I could think was that I must be making it up and that I was more selfish than I had thought. I ended my morning time that day with more questions than answers.

The next day I asked again, and I heard the same thing: "I love you." In that moment as I sat with that response, I asked, "Am I what you are thinking about? " The response was: "Yes!"

Never in my wildest dream did I think there was a possibility that it was me--He was thinking about. For a long time when I had asked the question "What are You thinking about?" He had wanted to talk about me.

As you ask this question, remember that He is not locked into some of our repetitive ways of thinking and that He is far more interested in you than you can imagine.

Day 21 Journaling

Sit in a comfortable spot and ask God what He is thinking about right now.

Write about your encounter below.

_____

_____

_____

_____

_____

_____

_____

_____

_____

_____

Day 22 - Breaking News!

When you go to bed, ask Holy Spirit for a headline and ask where to find it.

Genesis 20:3 (AMPC) "But God came to Abimelech in a dream by night and said, Behold, you are a dead man because of the woman whom you have taken [as your own], for she is a man's wife."

Job 33:14-18 (AMPC) "For God [does reveal His will;He] speaks not only once, but more than once, even though men do not regard it [including you, Job]. [One may hear God's voice] in a dream, in a vision of the night, when deep sleep falls on men while slumbering upon the bed, Then He opens the ears of men and seals their instruction [terrifying them with warnings], That He may withdraw man from his purpose and cut off pride from him [disgusting him with his own disappointing self-sufficiency]. He holds him back from the pit [of destruction], and his life from perishing by the sword [of God's destructive judgments]."

This activation is kind of tricky, or it has been for me in the past. On numerous occasions, I would be laying in bed and think I had heard something; or in a dream, I would see a headline for the next morning. When I woke up, I would start looking through news feeds and websites only to discover there was no such headline.

This became a source of discouragement and frustration. I was confused about whether I actually could hear God or not. This went on for a few weeks. Then one day, when I thought I had seen a headline, instead of looking at news feeds, I just sat and asked, "What am I seeing, and where can I find it?" A "soft" feeling deep inside nudged me to Facebook. Sure enough, when I opened Facebook, there was the headline. I was so focused on searching the news, I had never imagined the headline might be found somewhere other than a news outlet.

Our Father is inviting us into a life with Him. In that invitation comes the ability to be intertwined throughout a process, not to just hear and do what we are told. We can ask questions and understand "..it is the glory of kings to search out a matter."

Music would seem to be a natural form of communication in heaven if you read through scripture. I believe He loves all forms, types and styles of music. I find that many times when I am asking what will be playing on the radio, that a song will start playing in my head. That song is often   what will be playing when I turn on a device to listen to music. I have also found that the song has a message from Him to me. His love is amazing and His kindness everlasting. Both of which He tells me through the songs He "plays" for me.

By the way, if you are wondering, I am listening to Fred Hammond and Kirk Franklin as I write this. Have fun! Enjoy this exercise and listen because the echo of His voice is there.

Day 22 Journaling

When you go to bed, ask Holy Spirit for a headline and ask where to find it.

Write about your encounter below.

_____

_____

_____

_____

_____

_____

_____

_____

_____

_____

_____

Day 23 - Mountains, Oceans, and Deserts

Go outside and ask questions about creation. Ask such questions as "How did you create a pine tree? What were you thinking when you created it?"

Romans 1:20 (AMPC)"For ever since the creation of the world His invisible nature and attributes, that is, His eternal power and divinity, have been made intelligible and clearly discernible in and through the things that have been made (His handiworks). So [men] are without excuse [altogether without any defense or justification],"

Job 12:7-10 (NKJV) "But now ask the beasts, and they will teach you; And the birds of the air, and they will tell you; Or speak to the earth, and it will teach you; And the fish of the sea will explain to you. Who among all these does not know That the hand of the Lord has done this, In whose hand is the life of every living thing, And the breath of all mankind?"

Colossians 1:16 (NKJV)"For by Him all things were created that are in heaven and that are on earth, visible and invisible, whether thrones or dominions or principalities or powers. All things were created through Him and for Him."

The quiet of the forest.

The crashing waves of the ocean.

The sunset in the desert.

These are examples of moments where it is impossible not to see the beauty of our Father's work. Many times, I find myself staring at a tree, amazed and in awe of its life system: the layers of the tree, it's root system, and even the way each one is unique though it is from the same family. At these moments, I find myself asking about the creativity that inspired such a creation. Oftentimes, these awe-inspiring moments lead me to a place of personal creativity.

As you go outside, take in the wonders around you and allow Him to take you into your own creative experience.

Day 23 Journaling

Go outside and ask questions about creation. Ask such questions as "How did you create a pine tree? What were you thinking when you created it?"

Write about your encounter below.

_____

_____

_____

_____

_____

_____

_____

_____

_____

Day 24 - Just for Fun

Ask for His thoughts on your hobby or interest and if He would like to join you while you do it.

Psalm 40:5 (NKJV) "Many, O Lord my God, are Your wonderful works Which You have done; And Your thoughts toward us Cannot be recounted to You in order; If I would declare and speak of them, They are more than can be numbered."

Psalm 139:17-18 (NASB) "How precious also are Your thoughts to me, O God! How vast is the sum of them! If I should count them, they would outnumber the sand. When I awake, I am still with You."

Years ago, I was an avid basketball player. There was a time I played seven days a week and traveled everywhere with shorts and a ball. I loved basketball. Blowing by someone. Hitting a jump shot over an outstretched arm. Stealing a pass. Blocking a shot. That last second shot dropping in. The look on a person's face because they underestimate my abilities. Even now in my heart, I believe I have one more game in me. Yep, I love the game.

Well, it wasn't long into being married that seven days a week no longer worked. Life was changing, and my relationship with God was changing. I found myself playing less, praying more, and spending time at home was more of a priority.

It was an interesting time and I remember asking God if basketball was a bad thing and if I should quit. There was a loud, "No!"

Because of my love for the game, I believed that what I heard was really my own heart response, and I would need help trying to figure it out.

I didn't trust Shannon to give a fair answer, so I approached a friend and told him I was asking God about quitting basketball. He looked at me and in true friend fashion said, "Thats stupid!" (I would later come to find out that he had also heard God say, "No," and that's why he had relayed the message to me.)

Realizing I couldn't play if I wanted to without talking to Shannon, I went and asked her thoughts. She looked at me and said, "Why would God take something from you that you love if it's not sin or causing harm?" I was stunned. I had never considered that.

I signed up for the next league I could find. As I played, I found myself having conversations with Him throughout the game and playing really well. It was the most fun I had ever had in a league.

I truly believe Holy Spirit loves being invited to hang out with us as we do the things we love. So, enjoy this time with Him!

Day 24 Journaling

Ask for His thoughts on your hobby or interest and if He would like to join you while you do it.

Write about your encounter below.

_____

_____

_____

_____

_____

_____

_____

_____

_____

_____

Day 25 - Holy Spirit Art Critic

Find a painting and ask His opinion.

Psalm 19:1 (AMPC) "The heavens declare the glory of God; and the firmament shows and proclaims His handiwork"

Ecclesiastes 3:11 (AMPC) "He has made everything beautiful in its time. He also has planted eternity in men's hearts and minds [a divinely implanted sense of a purpose working through the ages which nothing under the sun but God alone can satisfy], yet so that men cannot find out what God has done from the beginning to the end"

Psalm 50:1-2 (NIV) "The Mighty One, God, the Lord, speaks and summons the earth from the rising of the sun to where it set."

As you gaze and ponder the work of the artist, what an amazing moment to talk to the Master Painter about creativity He has planted in this artist. That moment brings you to a place in the conversation where you can't be sure what He is more excited about: the creation or the creator of the creation.

As I have done this exercise, I have often found Him talking about the creator of the piece of art rather than the art itself. How awesome is it to talk to the Father about the artist. As He shares new perspectives and points out nuances of the creation, art can take on a whole new meaning, allowing us to move into places of revelation and encounter because of people's incredible gifts from heaven.

Day 25 Journaling

Find a painting and ask His opinion.

Write about your encounter below.

_____

_____

_____

_____

_____

_____

_____

_____

_____

_____

Day 26 - A Walk to Remember

Go on a walk with Jesus.

Genesis 5:24 (KJV) "And Enoch walked with God; and he was not, for God took him."

Genesis 6:9 (NKJV) "This is the genealogy of Noah. Noah was a just man, perfect in his generations. Noah walked with God."

On my most recent walk with God, I just held out my hand as if He were next to me and would want to hold my hand and then began to walk. As I walked, He talked to me about my family, how He loves them and how excited He is about how the kids are growing up so well. Then He started talking to me about when my mom was alive, reminding me about things that had happened and how funny they were. As we walked, joy grew within me. It felt the same as going on a walk with my friend, my kids, or my wife.

God's original intention has always been to have us walk with Him. He has been giving us the option to return to Him since Adam and Eve left the garden. Take Him up on His offer and listen to what He shares.

Day 26 Journaling

Go on a walk with Jesus.

Write about your encounter below.

_____

_____

_____

_____

_____

_____

_____

_____

_____

_____

Day 27 - Movie Night with Dad

Invite God to watch a movie with you. Ask Him what He wants to see and talk about the movie as you view it together.

James 4:8 (NKJV) "Draw near to God and He will draw near to you."

Proverbs 8:17 (NIV) "I love those who love me, and those who seek me find me."

Watching a movie together with God is an opportunity just to enjoy time in each other's presence and to see how He admires creativity. It is also a time to hear His thoughts and insights which can become quite the revelatory experience.

In 2000, a movie starring Russell Crowe came out called Gladiator. As the movie began, Crowe's character was about to lead his men into combat. He was giving his men instructions and said: "What we do here echoes in eternity." This line struck me to my core, and I actually yelled in response to the line during the scene.

During the rest of the film, I had a conversation about how He is Alpha and Omega. The concept of being part of eternity took a whole new meaning for me after that line. It was as if God had something He wanted to share, and it was in a theater He chose to share a piece of Himself I hadn't seen before.

Who knew you could have a movie date with God?

Day 27 Journaling

Invite God to watch a movie with you. Ask Him what He wants to see and talk about the movie as you view it together.

Write about your encounter below.

_____

_____

_____

_____

_____

_____

_____

_____

_____

_____

Day 28 - What's on the Menu?

Ask Holy Spirit what you should eat for a meal or for the day.

Genesis 9:3 (NKJV) "Every moving thing that lives shall be food for you; and as I gave you the green vegetables and plants, I give you everything."

John 4:34 (NKJV) "Jesus said to them, "My food is to do the will of Him who sent Me, and to finish His work."

Matthew 6:16-18 (NKJV) "And whenever you are fasting, do not look gloomy and sour and dreary like the hypocrites, for they put on a dismal countenance, that their fasting may be apparent to and seen by men. Truly I say to you, they have their reward in full already. But when you fast, perfume your head and wash your face, So that your fasting may not be noticed by men but by your Father, Who sees in secret; and your Father, Who sees in secret, will reward you in the open."

I have found this to be what I consider a loaded question/ exercise. Multiple times I have asked this question and found myself in a conversation about feasting. Scripture actually talks more about feasting than it talks about fasting. Who knew? I don't remember any church I have been a part of or connected with calling for a church wide feast--unless you count the church potluck.

What has been so interesting about this exercise has been the questions it has led to as well as some of His unique answers.

There have been times I've gone to a fast-food place because He wanted me to talk with someone there or just spent time in my car with Him not eating, no food even though I had bought lunch. Conversation and being present--these are far more important than we realize. That is all this exercise is. No worries about getting it wrong, just practice being present with Him and getting to know Him.

Day 28 Journaling

Ask Holy Spirit what you should eat for a meal or for the day.

Write about your encounter below.

_____

_____

_____

_____

_____

_____

_____

_____

_____

_____

Day 29 - World Traveler

Get a world map and ask, "If I could be anywhere right now, where would I want to be"

Isaiah 6:3 (AMPC)"And one cried to another and said, Holy, holy, holy is the Lord of hosts; the whole earth is full of His glory!"

Psalm 145:18 (NASB)"The Lord is near to all who call upon Him, To all who call upon Him in truth."

Leviticus 26:11-12 (AMPC)"I will set My dwelling in and among you, and My soul shall not despise or reject or separate itself from you. And I will walk in and with and among you and will be your God, and you shall be My people."

It may seem like a weird question to ask someone that is everywhere, and in places you are not or even imagined, "Where do you want to be?"

This is the type of question you ask when you begin to realize who you are and your personal importance to your Father. This exercise will help you discover pieces of His heart that you may not have dreamed of, places He loves to "visit". You can discover what He wants to speak over a place like Vacaville or just finding a peaceful park that He loves to sit at. This activation is about searching His heart and finding places He loves to be.

What would He want me to say over a city like Hong Kong. Going to a place He leads you and hearing what He says about it gives you a glimpse of His reality. This is an opportunity to explore His heart for places all over the earth and to really lean into His gracious, merciful and kind heart for those places.

Day 29 Journaling

Get a world map and ask, "If I could be anywhere right now, where would I want to be"

Write about your encounter below.

_____

_____

_____

_____

_____

_____

_____

_____

_____

_____

Day 30 - Getaway

Plan a vacation for the two of you.

Mark 6:31-32 (NKJV) "And He said to them, "Come aside by yourselves to a deserted place and rest a while." For there were many coming and going, and they did not even have time to eat. So they departed to a deserted place in the boat by themselves."

Song of Solomon 2:10 (NKJV) "My beloved spoke, and said to me: "Rise up, my love, my fair one, And come away."

This is such a fun thing to do. First, just the idea of a vacation gets me excited. Where does your imagination go?

It has been a few years since I have gone on a vacation with Him (or the family for that matter). The last time was in the Fall about three years ago, and it was more of a *staycation* with isolation, so it was just us. I spent time locked in a room alone with activities only meant to create space for an encounter with Him. This opportunity was more refreshing than anything I had ever done up to that point or since. This experience brought me to a place of new clarity and also created in me a deeper desire to know Him more. An incredible byproduct of this time was that it ultimately left me wanting more. This vacation with Him was incredible, and I came away knowing Him more while also opening my eyes to how much more of Him I don't know. But what a beautiful cycle.

Day 30 Journaling

Plan a vacation for the two of you.

Write about your encounter below.

_____

_____

_____

_____

_____

_____

_____

_____

_____

_____

Final Thoughts

As you conclude this thirty day journey, I'd like to talk a little more about how these different activations have influenced me and also speak about what comes next.

For many of you, these activations may have seemed normal or even elementary. For others, the activations may have felt uncomfortable or even paralyzed you by being way outside of your current paradigm. In either case, hopefully, you have found a fresh way to encounter Holy Spirit and to build a relationship with your heavenly Father that is outside of the paradigm others have created.

For me, these activations have been an integral part of learning how to hear as well as breaking down mental barriers that kept me from knowing Him and living in the fullness of who I was created to be. Many of these I have continued for consecutive days until Holy Spirit wanted me to change up and do something new. However, I still regularly ask for divine appointments and pretty regularly ask about what to wear. There are others and variations of some I still use semi-regularly. What I pray you have experienced is that each activation or your version of them has led you into a new place. A place without boundaries or restrictions.

As you move on from this thirty days, please know that repetition and journaling of these activations are what has helped me develop my prophetic gifting as well as stirred my passion for His presence. I encourage you to continue your pursuit of Him, which always unlocks everything He has for you.

If you feel that you have moved beyond the activations within the book, check my website or Facebook for other training and teachings that may help on your journey. Ultimately, I train, teach, prophesy, and speak all that I have been entrusted to release. But if you want the short cut, the cheat code so to speak, it is scripture that has everything you are looking for. Scripture tells us that the Holy Spirit will lead us and guide us into all truth. Sometimes that is by connecting us to individuals, communities, or even just leading us to a training. In the end, there is no substitute for learning His voice and how to follow Him.

Enjoy the Journey!

Excelsior - Upward and onward to greater glory!

Activations

1. Get your Bible and ask Holy Spirit for a verse for your day.

2. Get your Bible and ask Holy Spirit for a verse for a friend or family member.

3. Have a meal with Holy Spirit. Set a place and expect to have a conversation like you would if your friend was sitting at the table with you.

4. Ask Holy Spirit what to read and read it together.

5. Ask Holy Spirit what will be the next type of communication you will receive: a phone call, text message, email, Facebook message, etc.?

6. Ask Holy Spirit what song will be on the radio when you get in the car.

7. Ask Holy Spirit who will be the first person you see today?

8. Before you go out for coffee, a snack, lunch or dinner, ask Holy Spirit for the server's gender, age or name.

9. If you have a meeting or are going out with a friend, ask Holy Spirit the first ting they will say?

10. Before you get dressed each day ask Holy Spirit what clothes you should wear, then watch for something about your outfit to be mentioned during the day.

Activations

11. Go for a drive and ask God where to go.

12. Ask Holy Spirit to go on a ride with you and just drive and talk.

13. Put on some worship music and ask God to let you hear the worship of heaven.

14. Go to a store with numbered aisles and ask God what aisle to go to and who will be there. Ask for details about the person: man, woman, old, young. This exercise has many options for you to experiment with.

15. Ask Holy Spirit for a message for a specific person you will come in contact with that day.

16. Put on some music and ask God for a dance.

17. Start your morning by saying out loud "Good Morning" and wait for His response.

18. Go to a public place and ask God what His favorite thing is about this place.

19. Play a game together: video game, phone game, or board game.

20. Ask God, "What do you think about me?"

Activations

21. Sit in a comfortable spot and ask God what He is thinking about right now.

22. When you go to bed, ask Holy Spirit for a headline and ask where to find it.

23. Go outside and ask questions about creation. Ask such questions as "How did you create a pine tree? What were you thinking when you created it?"

24. Ask for His thoughts on your hobby or interest and if He would like to join you while you do it.

25. Find a painting and ask His opinion.

26. Go on a walk with Jesus.

27. Invite God to watch a movie with you. Ask Him what He wants to see and talk about the movie as you view it together.

28. Ask Holy Spirit what you should eat for a meal or for the day.

29. Get a world map and ask, "If I could be anywhere right now, where would I want to be"

30. Plan a vacation for the two of you.

STAY CONNECTED

Website & Newsletter

LEGACYDREAMERS.ORG

Instagram

@LEGACYDREAMERS

Facebook

/LEGACYDREAMERS

Contact Us: Admin@LegacyDreamers.org

About the Author

Craig Farris is the co-founder of Legacy Dreamers Ministries. He and his wife Shannon are the visionaries and leaders of this nonprofit organization, where they share the Father's heart for His people by speaking identity, destiny, and strategic words for people, businesses, churches, governments, and institutions. Craig is a prophetic voice to many and believes that anyone can prophesy. His heart is to teach people the art of hearing God and releasing them into their original purpose. Craig, Shannon, and their twelve children currently reside in Cedar Park, TX.

Made in the USA
Columbia, SC
22 July 2022

63816197R00102